ANCIENT EGYPT

Egypt currently exists.

It is a country located in the Northeast of Africa.

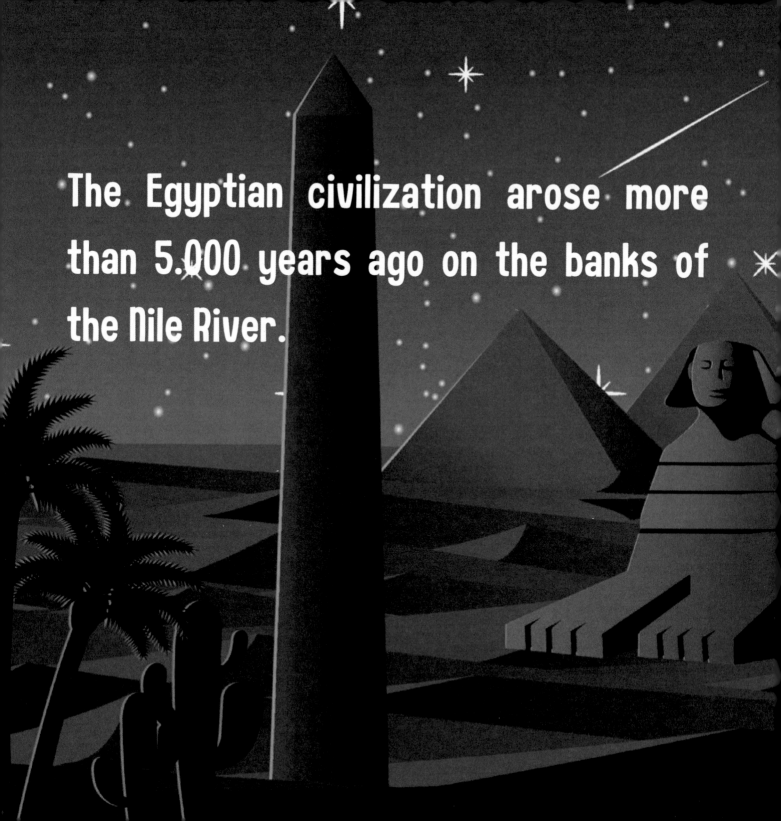

The Egyptian civilization arose more than 5,000 years ago on the banks of the Nile River.

And lasted more than 3000 years.

There were originally two kingdoms:
- Upper Egypt
- Lower Egypt

King Narmer united the two kingdoms, thus becoming the first pharaoh of Ancient Egypt and founder of the First Dynasty.

Ancient Egypt began on the banks of the Nile River, around 3100 B.C.

The Nile is the largest river in Africa and the second largest in the world.

It has a length of almost 7000 km.

That means a large amount of water to drink, farm, keep animals...

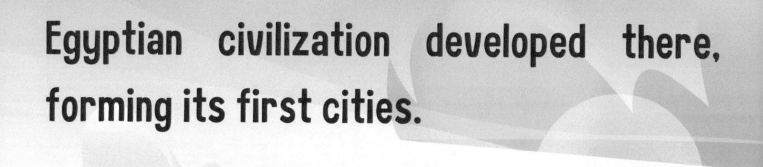

Egyptian civilization developed there, forming its first cities.

Ancient Egypt was almost all desert.

The banks of the Nile River were the only fertile lands where they could farm.

The waters of the Nile River allowed navigation, as roads, thus facilitating the transportation of goods, animals, building supplies, people...

Egyptians worshiped several gods.

It is what is known as polytheism (belief in more than one god).

Some of these gods had the head of an animal and the body of a person.

One of the most important gods was Ra, the god of the Sun.

But there were many more. Some of them were...

Osiris

Isis

Horus

God of religion and agriculture.

Goddess of motherhood.

God of war and hunting.

Amon

God of creation.

Anubis

God of death and resurrection.

Seth

God of the desert.

The pharaohs were the kings of Ancient Egypt.

They were considered representatives of the gods.

One of the best-known pharaohs is Tutankhamun, who was pharaoh when he was only 9 years old.

Howard Carter discovered his tomb in 1922.

The most famous monuments in Egypt are the pyramids.

They were funerary temples, that is, tombs for the pharaohs.

Egyptians believed in life after death.

They mummified the bodies of the pharaohs to preserve them in the afterlife.

The mummies were placed in decorated sarcophagi.

And, since they believed in the afterlife, the pharaohs were buried with objects that could be taken with them after death.

To build each pyramid, the work of thousands of workers was needed for years.

Inside the pyramids, they built tunnels, passageways, and secret chambers.

The most famous monuments of Egypt are located in Giza, and they are:

Khafre

Cheops

Menkaure

The three primary pyramids...

...and the Great Sphinx of Giza.

Hieroglyphs were the writing system invented by the ancient Egyptians.

They consisted in the representation of words through signs and figures.

They were a big mystery until Champollion managed to decipher them through the Rosetta stone, in 1822.

The ancient Egyptians tamed animals.

They kept cats, dogs, and monkeys as pets.

Cats were venerated in Ancient Egypt.

One of the most important goddesses was Bastet, represented in the form of a domestic cat or a cat-headed woman.

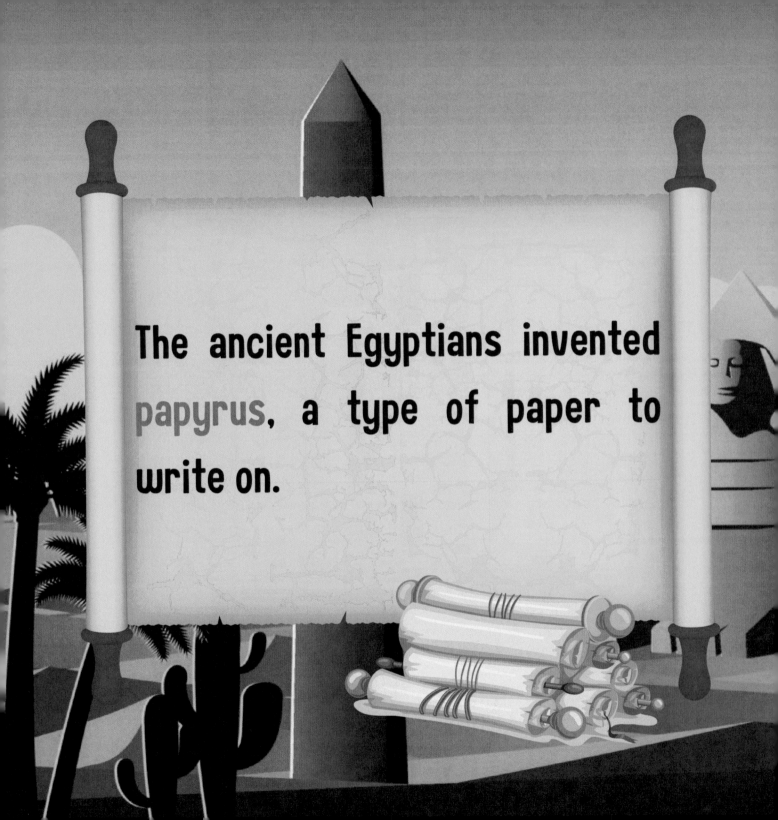

The ancient Egyptians invented papyrus, a type of paper to write on.

They also invented things like the sundial, makeup, cosmetics, and the solar calendar, among many other things.

And here it ends!

I hope you liked it and learned new things.

Until next time!

I want to ask you a favor so that this book reaches more people, and that is that you rate it with a sincere opinion on the platform where you purchased it.

With that small gesture, you will be helping me to carry on with new projects.

I can't wait to start creating my next book for you!

See you soon!

ANCIENT EGYPT

VOLCANOES for Kids

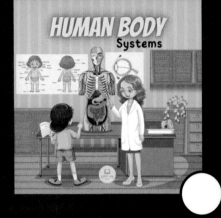

HUMAN BODY Systems

THE MOST FAMOUS Landmarks IN THE WORLD

FASCINATING UNIVERSE

THE WATER CYCLE For Kids

DINOSAURS

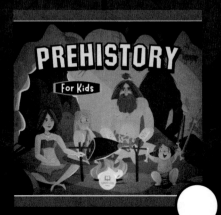

PREHISTORY For Kids

SCAN ME

I HAVE A GIFT FOR YOU!

This Free eBook is for You!

SCAN ME

https://www.bit.ly/samueljohngift

I HOPE YOU LIKE IT!

Samuel John

BOOKS

 contacto@samueljohnbooks.com

 www.facebook.com/bookssamueljohn/

 FOLLOW ME

www.amazon.com/author/samueljohnbooks

Made in the USA
Middletown, DE
05 September 2023